THE TIME OF BARBARIANS

St. Quodvultdeus

Bishop of Carthage

Translated by: D.P. Curtin

Dalcassian
Publishing
Company

THE TIME OF BARBARIANS

Copyright @ 2009 Dalcassian Publishing Company

All rights reserved. No part of this publication may be reproduced, distributed, or transmitted in any form or by any means, including photocopying, recording, or other electronic or mechanical methods, without the prior written permission of the publisher, except in the case of brief quotations embodied in critical reviews and certain other non-commercial uses permitted by copyright law. For permission request, write to Dalcassian Publishing Company at dalcassianpublishing at gmail.com

ISBN: 979-8-8692-8602-4 (Paperback)

Library of Congress Control Number:
Author: Curtin, D.P. (1985-)

Printed by Ingram Content Group, 1 Ingram Blvd, La Vergne, Tennessee

First printing edition 2009.

THE TIME OF BARBARIANS

THE TIMEOF THE BARBARIANS

CHAPTER I

1. That repentance should be embraced when God scourges for sins. By the scourge of God all are deservedly crushed. The Lord our God reminds us that we should not neglect our sins when he shows such anger. For he himself justly punishes the guilty, because he finds no one who repents. How often, dearest, have the divine trumpets sounded and are sounding: Do penance; Has the kingdom of heaven drawn near to you (Matt. 4:17)? And with the ears of the heart closed, we work more on evil, and ask that good things may come. But the apostle says that such a judgment is just. For in the very fact that those who are like that think that they can receive good things from bad works, they are hardened, and require no place for repentance. Those who are found to be condemned by themselves deserve to be judged justly. Although this speech of ours does not touch all, yet the divine word binds all, saying: All have declined,

at the same time they have become useless; there is no one who does good, there is not even one (Ps. 13:3). How all, and how not all? How could everyone not? Because there are many who groan and grieve because of the iniquities that are taking place in their midst, wanting to resist; but not daring for fear of worldly things, which human frailty still longs to gain, or weakness fears to lose. According to what they grieve, not all; because the fear of man is valued more than the fear of God, and men prefer the things which they have received from God to God himself. Lest an evil man take them away, God is despised, by whom man was made. I would indeed like you, who are still such, and to be bound by the love of worldly things, to either spare or favor those who sin; I would indeed like to remind you with some exhortations, what you ought to put before what matter: unless the river of tears compels us to mourn those who sin and do not want to do penance. If there were human affection in us, if there were a sense of compassion, we should weep, grieve and mourn the death of one man: with what tears, with what groans, with what lamentations should we be moved, when we mourn either the greatest part or almost the whole of a city? The patient is dear, and his vein foretells evil; all who love him are sick at the same time. If they see him smiling even in his near death, how do they feel that all hope of salvation has been removed from him, and they mourn him still alive as if he had deservedly died? In the midst of such straits, and at the very end of things, the whole province is placed, and spectacles are frequented every day: the blood of men is daily shed in the world, and the voices of the insane blare in the circus. O weeping is more acceptable than all sorrow! O weeping, afflicting the heart with all sorrow! I like to cry. For we mourn, dearly beloved, both for them and for us, because we too are worthy to be scourged with such men. For us, when we accuse others; we have all declined, we have become useless at the same time, absolutely all of us. No one is excused; because he is such a judge that every man is found guilty by him. For when the just King sits on the throne, who will boast that he has a chaste heart? Or who will boast that he is clean from sin (Prov. 20:8-9)?

2. That time has come which the Lord foretold: Do you think that when the Son of Man comes, he will find faith on earth (Luke 18:8)? Who has faith? Who believes in words? Will any one of us dare to assign faith to himself, when he hears the Lord saying to his disciples: If you had faith like a grain of mustard seed, you would say to this tree, Be uprooted and planted in the sea; and would

he have obeyed you (Luke 17:6)? Who will dare to assign to himself that he does all that God has commanded? No one, absolutely no one. We preach, and do not do: you hear, and do not care to do. All deserve to be under the scourge, both the teacher and the doer, and the listener and the despiser. We tend to criticize each other, and we don't tend to discuss our works. Neighbor defrauds neighbor, cleric defrauds cleric, layman defrauds layman. I see them accusing each other, but I don't see anyone just apologizing. For each one, dearest, bears his own burden. Do not detract from one another, brothers, says the Apostle James. For he who detracts from his brother or judges his brother, detracts from the law and judges the law. But if you judge the law, you are not the maker of the law, but the judge. For there is one lawgiver and judge, who can destroy and save. But who are you to judge your neighbor (Jam. 4:11-13)?

CHAPTER II.

3. Repentance to be done before the tree is cut down. And yet the voices of the detractors cannot be silenced by the word of God. He cries out through the good and through the bad: Repent, the kingdom of God has drawn near to you. Do not be hearers of the law only, but doers (Jam. 1:22). Be worthy of the fruits of repentance. For behold, says the Evangelist, the ax is laid at the roots of the trees. For every tree that does not bear good fruit will be cut down and thrown into the fire (Matt. 3:2, 8-10). I see, says he, that all men are different trees, and have different fruits: but good fruit is sought by him that feedeth, not by him that pricketh. For there are also thorny trees, assigned to fire, and deservedly to be burned, because in them there is no fruit of the soul. Do you think, dearly beloved, that we are all such, who have been released into these evils for our sins? The farmer sharpens his iron, cuts down the useless wood, saves the cut to be burned in the fire. This is now being done by a true farmer. Indeed, it seems to them that evil still stands, still flourishes. Whoever you are like this, whoever you are bad, whoever you do not want to be corrected, you will not be comforted by your height; because a greater fall awaits you, and a greater flame supports you. Because this ax has not yet come to you, do you think you can stand forever? when you see or hear that other trees have fallen that are bigger than you. The reason why this farmer puts you off is his patience, lest perhaps a place of repentance should intervene with him. For that colonist in the Gospel, who interceded for the tree which the Lord wanted to

uproot, because it had not borne fruit for three years, see what he said: Lord, let it go this year too; I will make a ditch for it, I will use a basket of dung: if it bears fruit, well; but if not, cut it off (Luke 13:8, 9). This barren tree is a kind of people who do not have the fruit of repentance. He is its master, its founder. The apostle Paul is the intercessor of this tree. Where do we prove it? Hear in one of his Epistles how he interceded for such: I bend my knees, he says. the Father of our Lord Jesus Christ, that he may give you strength (Eph. 3:14, 16). Therefore, he asked them to receive what they did not have. I will make him a ditch, he said, and I will use a basket of dung. The pit is the place of humility: the basket of dung, the tears of the penitent. If anyone despises that place, he will bear the cannon any longer, when he has felt the sharpest tool of that farmer. Repent, you evil ones; correct the wicked, for the good are also scourged with you.

CHAPTER III.

4. Why should the good be punished with the bad? Someone will say: If the bad are deservedly scourged, why do the good suffer such things with the bad and from the bad? Why? Because according to a certain manner they are called good; but according to what is right and true and good, no one is good but God alone (Luke 18:19). Therefore the good themselves, whoever are good, are not such as the good ought to be: for they are not perfect good; for they progress from day to day. If they are successful, of course they are successful in their training. No one will justify himself as if he were already perfect. Let the Pelagian justifier depart from the midst, let the Arian heretic be confounded: for there is none good but God alone. What then? Is Christ not God? Clearly God. For the divine Scripture says of him: This is the true God and eternal life (1 John 5:20). What is the Holy Spirit, is not God? Clearly God. How do we prove that it is God himself? Hear in the Acts of the Apostles Peter rebuking Ananias the deceiver: Ananias said, why has satan filled your heart, that you should lie to the Holy Spirit? You have not lied to men, but to God (Acts 5:3-4). Behold, and the Holy Spirit, God. Therefore, the Trinity is one God: and it is true that no one is good but one God. Be patient, good, that you may be truly good: be patient until the coming of the Lord. Bear the evils which you suffer from evils with evils; because this temptation is your examination. If you are gold, why are you afraid of straw, why are you afraid of fire? You will indeed be

in the furnace together, but the fire turns the straw into ashes and removes the dirt from you. If you are corn, why are you afraid of the tribe? You will not appear as you were before in the spike, unless the thresher separates the chaff from you by crushing it. If you are oil, what are you afraid of press pressure? Your appearance will not be revealed unless the weight of a stone separates you from the sea. Nevertheless, let each soul question itself, and see if it suffers unjustly. Let the balance of justice be brought forward, let the love of the world be weighed with the love of God, see how the love of the world will prevail. The mirror of the divine Scriptures is brought forth. This mirror does not touch anyone: it shows you what you are. Look and see, and if there is anything that offends, go away confused and come back corrected. Will you not be ashamed, and glory in your evils? For you will be perfect evil, and not any kind of good. Do you not want to be scourged with the world, or do you grumble under the scourge when you are scourged? Poor servant, did you do what the Lord commanded? Lest you be scourged, those scourges he foretold you before. Who commanded? The Lord commanded, your Creator commanded. What did he order? He who loves father or mother more than me, he says, is not worthy of me. Behold what he commanded. Or, He who loves a son or a daughter more than me is not worthy of me (Matt. 10:37). Behold what he commanded. And who, he says, hates father or mother or children? Nor did he command them to be hated: but he commanded himself to be loved as much as them. Indeed, you ought to love the Creator more than the creature; but if you are not able to prefer it, at least deign to equal it. You would truly love your children, if you preferred Christ to your children, and committed your children to themselves. You would truly love your children if you loved them in Him who gave them to you to love. Do you therefore seem to love them, because you favor their pleasures? You hear those who blaspheme, and bear it patiently, Christian, because King Nebuchadnezzar could not endure foreigners, saying: If anyone blasphemes against God, Shadrach, Misach, and Abednego shall be destroyed (Dan. 3:96). You see, you attend shows, and you don't call back. You see them luxuriant, and you do not beat them. Nor can you present yourself as such a father, who is ready to either disinherit or cast away undisciplined children, when you ought to have been ready, like Abraham, to sacrifice even his son. For every one who slaughters the pleasures of his children offers a sacrifice such as Abraham offered to God. But as long as these things do not take place, and those who use this world are badly nourished by these depraved morals, the world will collapse, and it is not without merit that the prophet says: The earth will sink away, and all who dwell in it (Is. 24:4). Even now men do not cease to murmur, to praise the past times, to accuse the Christian times. The times of our fathers were great, they say: O what good times our fathers had!

CHAPTER IV

5. Each one will chastise and punish the faults in his own by the example of the ancients. But look at what our fathers did. Phinehas killed a man sacrificing to idols with his own hand, in order to appease the wrath of God (Num. 25:8). Moses rebuked the wandering people, worshiping the burnt calf, with such a sure correction that, calling to him one of the twelve tribes that wanted to follow God, he gave them a command that, taking swords in their hands, the children should strike the parents, and the parents should kill the children (Exod. 32:26-28). No emotion recalled them, no place was reserved for humanity; because the fear and love of God prevailed over all the love of carnal desires. Jephthah, in order to overcome his enemies sacrificing to the gods and demons, gave his only daughter as a sacrifice (Jud. 11). When Samson, with the power which he had received from God in his head, had crushed and worn out the demonic nations for a long time with wars, and had afterwards been seduced by a woman, he had lost his eyes and the strength of his head at the same time, after he had learned that they had all come together to the temple of their idols to their shame, and to magnify them as their gods, because to them they had betrayed their fiercest enemy, when the hair of his head had grown on him, and he had the courage to ask the boy who had given him guidance to give him his hand, and he asked to be led to that temple. When he had arrived at this, he took hold of the two columns, on which the whole building was carried, each in his hands, and wished to crush himself and them together with the fall, so that the praises of the demons would not be heard by anyone willingly as an insult to his God (Jud. 16). Daniel did not ask any request from a human king, but from the living God, who guarantees all his goods, he was given to the fasting lions to perish. He fed the lions (Dan. 14:30-40). What shall I say of the three boys, who, refusing to worship the royal image, laughed at the fires? In which children a shining grace so shone, that they were thrown into the furnace bound, and were seen walking, opening their mouths and praising God, not admitting the flames to themselves, but fleeing: that they deserved to

have the Son of God with them, before he appeared to the world in man; that a flame might be their avenger, and a devouring furnace consume the ministers of the Chaldeans; and being produced unscathed from the furnace, they would make the people marvel at themselves, and change the king, and make him a worshiper of their God, whom they had previously felt to be a persecutor (Dan. 3). But faith, fear, and love of God did all these things. They hated not only all that they had for God's sake; but also their souls: and God made them famous here and enriched them with the reward of eternal life. What, beloved, have we done, nay, on the contrary, what evils have we not done? They sacrificed to the demons neither by threats nor by torture. Did he not sacrifice, who willingly looked at the images of the idols playing during the night, which they call Nocturne? He sacrificed, completely sacrificed; and what is worse, not the victim of a bull or any cattle, but the very precious soul of man. In this so unholy sacrifice, not one or a few are accused; The whole city did this, and all consented. Not by enemies, nor by barbarians, but by himself, every man in his soul kills himself within by seeing, consenting, not preventing; we all remained to the point: and while we do not want the peace of the state to be disturbed in a perverse way, we do not accept the right peace that we desire. We scorn to keep the peace of good manners, and the peace of our times has perished. Learn even now, beloved, what you ought to prioritize. Do not love faults in children, in friends, in servants, in all acquaintances. A singular power is preferred to all power; let us render honor to Caesar as to Caesar, and fear to God. The Creator of creation is to be preferred: let us love God because he loves us; and in that he thus scourges us, he loves. For who is the son whom his father does not discipline (Heb. 12:6, 7)? He who has a sound consideration, who believes in the words of God, fears eternal fire more than the sword of any savage barbarian; he fears eternal death, the worst death of any kind here. Let the unbelievers scoff at these things, let the fools scoff, they do not want to believe even in things they have experienced. Behold, they are crushed, behold, everything perishes, behold, the world which they loved cannot stand with them, behold, they are drawn to God, whose precepts they despised: for he does not continue with a good will, who dies blaspheming. Behold, he goes: when he comes thither, what is done? Where is he going? By whom will he go? Who is forced to return here again? It ended and he ended up making amends for what he had done wrong. Return, children, return; return, transgressors, to your heart (Is. 46:8): make joy from your conversion, let your hearts be corrected, let your works displease you. Be strong, let not the tribulation of the world break you: the Lord is near; do not be anxious about anything (Phil. 4:5-6).

CHAPTER V

6. The fortitude of the martyrs, namely Perpetua and Felicity. You have great examples of brave men. Martyrs conquered the world: among these martyrs, women were found to be stronger than men. A few days ago we celebrated the birthdays of the martyrs Perpetua and Felicity, and the count. And since there are so many men there, why are these two mentioned above all, except because the weaker sex has either equaled or surpassed the strength of the men? One of them was pregnant, the other was nursing. Felicity was giving birth, Perpetua was nursing. But this Perpetua nursed so long, as long as she received from that shepherd at the same time as her father a mouthful of milk: by which she accepted the sweetness of eternal happiness, which made her despise her son, reject her father, not cling to the world, and lose her soul for Christ. But Felicity, who had Perpetua as her companion, gave birth and was in pain; What virtue in women! What grace is there, which when it pours itself out, judges no unworthy sex! Thanks be to God: for he restored the female sex. The woman had remained in great disgrace; because from the beginning sin was through the woman, and because of her we all die. The devil cast down one Eve: but Christ, born of a virgin, exalted many women. Perpetua and Felicity trampled on the head of the serpent, which Eve admitted to her heart. He seduced her by making false promises; He was not able to overcome them by raging: he deceived her in the happiness of paradise; He could not go to these, nor was he placed under the power of so many. He enjoyed his fall among the delights of paradise; The devil himself, in a certain way, was afraid of the constancy of their courage among the punishments. They are deservedly so exalted, deservedly either equaled or preferred to men. For although in Christ Jesus there is neither slave nor free, there is neither male nor female (Gal. 3:28), but they are all one meeting the perfect man (Eph. 4:13); yet this gift came down from great grace. For 'Perpetual' and 'Happiness' are the names of these holy women, the reward of all the holy martyrs.

CHAPTER VI

7. Patience of Job. Even that Job, well known to all, conquered the world, having been tried many times, but by no means overcome. He fulfilled the Sunday precept: he despised the children, lest he should blaspheme the one who had given the children. He rejected his wife, who convinced him of blasphemy, whom the devil had therefore let alone because he knew that she was necessary to him. For he had not sent away a comforter for his husband, but a helper of his own temptation: he had made her a new Eve, but he was not the old Adam. He also thought that he could deceive him by means of a woman: but this one, by disputing the worst suggestive wife, with divine help, was able to overcome even the devil himself in her. Job was stronger in pain than Adam in the woods: he did not yield to tortures; he was overcome in pleasures. You see, beloved, what temptation does, how useful the pressures of this world are, and how earthly pleasures corrupt. Job despised his wife, his children, all that he had, and afterwards also his flesh. He loved those who had given more than what he had given. He used what he had received, like a good traveler: he possessed, he was not possessed. But when it pleased him to take them away, he who had blessed them, he did not blaspheme: the Lord, he says, gave, and the Lord took away; as it pleased the Lord, so it was done: blessed be the name of the Lord (Job 1-2). Imitate such a man, imitate such children who are also scourged, that they may be received. For he scourges every son whom he receives. Endure his discipline: as children, so God attacks you.

CHAPTER VII.

8. The parable of the prodigal son. The side of Christ is open, that all may enter through it. This is proved by the younger son placed in the Gospel, who despised his father's discipline, spent his substance on harlots, fed swine, was crushed by hunger, could not fill his belly with swine's pods: at last one day he returned to himself, and found himself the one who had lost himself. It occurred to him that many of his father's hired servants were abounding in bread, but he himself was dying of hunger. He rose immediately, ran back to his father, and asked to be counted not as a son, but as one of his servants. Humility is bowed down, compassion is aroused: the voices of the penitent son

shake the father's bowels. The son says that he is unworthy, that he may judge him worthy; he asks that he be ordered to be accepted among the servants: and his father orders that first robe to be brought to him, he slaughters a fatted calf, gathers a choir, calls on his friends, makes a great feast. Why? Because this son of mine, he said, had died, and has come to life; He was lost and found. The Lord proposed this similitude in the Gospel, which he himself explained, saying that such joy takes place in heaven over the sinner who does penance. But now, since it is time to exhort all to repentance, so that the erring children may return, and a feast may be prepared for them by the father's fattened calf, let us also, the most beloved, be ready to participate in this feast as friends and family; He now deigns to call us servants, but friends. Let us go over, if you please, the very parable proposed by the Lord in the Gospel, in which he showed us the affection of the pious father, and told of the return of the prodigal son, and of the elder son who had not left his father's house, he reported the troubled heart. Indeed, the text of the lesson itself has this. When his eldest son came from the field, he said, when he heard the symphony, he asked the servants what it was. And being indignant, he refused to enter. And his father went out to him to bring him in. And he reproached him with his father, because he had always worked with him, and had never shown him such things: but when that son came, who had spent all his father's substance badly, he killed a fatted calf for him. And the father gives the account of what he has done, and comforts his son, who remains with him, not leaving the house, and says to him, "Son, you are mine, and you are with me always, and everything is yours." , and revived; he was lost and was found (Luke 15:11-32). Such a proposal from the Lord is not empty. He therefore gives us who proposed these things, that we may show that this was fulfilled by him, that by a certain likeness he in a certain way aroused us to inquire into something. No Christian doubts that our Lord Jesus Christ showed a paternal affection to his own. Let us require more of him who is the younger son, who by living prodigally has squandered the father's substance, and who is the first-born son, who, indignant that the lost son's return was slaughtered with a stuffed calf, refuses to enter. Who is this prodigal son, who spent all his father's substance on harlots, if not the thief who, by pouring out the substance of his soul given to him by God, hanged it even on the cross? He fed the pigs when he fulfilled the pleasures of the demons by his deeds. Perhaps he fed those pigs whom the devil had asked the Lord, saying: Command us to enter into the herd of swine (Matt. 8:31). He was crushed by hunger, because he could not find the bread of God's word. He wanted to satiate his belly when he filled his soul with torturous thoughts. But let him return to himself, see himself hanging on the cross as a thief, run to his father, say as he hangs on the cross: Lord, remember me when you come into your kingdom. Lord, remember me; I am not worthy to be called your son, accept me as one of your servants. Lord, remember me. For, attending to his thief, he distrusted the merits of himself: but the Lord, like a pious father, offered to the thief, as if to a son, what he had despaired of. Let the father bring that first robe to him, clothe his son with immortality, whom he sees hanging on the cross with him, and bring him into the house: let Christ say to the thief, Amen, I say to you, today you will be with me in paradise (Luke 23:42, 43). He saw the fatted calf, the man who had been taken up, even crucified for the robbers. Let that banquet be prepared in heaven, let that choir of angels be present, sweetly declaring: Glory to God in the highest, and on earth peace to men of good will (Luke 2:14). Let that firstborn son also come, and he does not want to enter. Who is this first-born son who refused to enter, if not Peter, the first of the Apostles, who dared to deny the Lord three times to the questioning of one of the maids in the court of the priest? You indeed said, O Peter, as to your father Christ, I labored with you: when you said to the Savior, I am with you until death (Matt. 26:69-74, 35); I will lay down my life for you (John 13:37). Where is what you promised? You are asked once, and you deny it: you are asked a second time, and you deny it; thirdly, and you deny it. You do not want to enter the banquet, therefore you have dared to deny the Lord three times. Where is it, I will lay down my soul for you? The hooves did not frighten him who refused three times, but he crushed the little woman with one. Surely, I am with you until death. Look, look, then, Peter, how much you assumed about yourself before: behold, now, by denying three times, you are convinced by the rooster's witness. But let the father go out to the first-born son who does not want to enter: let Christ say to Peter, Enter into the joy of your Lord (Matt. 25:21). Let him look upon the denier and make him a confessor: let him reprove the weeper, and make him a lover. He exhorted him with a paternal voice: Son, he says, you are mine: you are Peter; though thou hast denied me, thou art mine. You are Peter, and on this rock I will build my church. You are mine, and all mine are yours: I will give you the keys of the kingdom of heaven (Matt. 16:18-19). With you, Peter, are the keys: deign to enter the banquet. It was necessary that these things should be done, since your brother had died as a thief, and had come back to life; He was lost and found. If Peter, before Christ was crucified for all, received the keys of the kingdom of heaven; By what means did that thief, who is no longer guilty, enter there, except through the side which the Jew opened?

9. And now let all come who love paradise, a place of rest, a place of security, a place of perpetual happiness, a place where you do not fear the barbarian, where you suffer no adversary, have no enemy: come all, enter all; it is where you can enter, the open side. For he showed the thief into which all must enter, and by his example taught no one to despair.

CHAPTER VIII.

Concerning the avoidance of the Arian heresy.--Strive, says the Lord, to enter through the narrow gate (Luke 13:24). What is narrower than that hole which one of the soldiers opened by striking the side of the crucified? and yet almost the whole world has already entered through these straits. Come, you Jews, the Son of God calls you whom you crucified. Strive to enter by the narrow gate: for by this your fathers entered. Those who cried out that he should be crucified, who saw him hanged on a tree, who laughed, who shook their heads, still entered through these difficulties. For it was not in vain that he cried out while hanging on the cross: Father, forgive them, for they know not what they do (Luke. 23:34). Through these, as I have said, straits, through the narrow gate of the side of Christ, a changed thief entered, a repentant Jew, every pagan was converted, and from him the evil Arian heretic went out. He went out, because it was not about the permanent number. For he was of those of whom John says: They went out from us, but they were not of us: for if they had been of us, they would certainly have remained with us (1 John 2:19). O Arian heretic, he recognizes the thief hanging on the cross, the very enemies of the Jews are afraid of the risen one, and you mistreat the one reigning in heaven!

10. Beware, beloved, of the Arian pestilence; they will not separate you from Christ by promising earthly things, they will not rob you of faith because of the garment Members of Christ, keep the unity and integrity of the one coat, which not even the persecutors of Christ dared to tear. Do not heap insults on your head: he died for you, that you should not die. Whom Christ quickened

by Baptism, why did the Arian kill him by rebaptizing him? Be ashamed, be ashamed, heretic. Peter refused, and returned, and with tears he wiped out what he had refused out of fear. Paul persecuted Christ among his people, but at his voice he fell and arose. In one way he fell, in another he rose: the persecutor fell, the preacher was raised. Among the Christians, the kings persecuted Christ: but they did much for them, when the members quickly passed to their head. No one inflicts such damages on Christ as you do: for you desire to kill the souls of many, for whom Christ came in the flesh to be slain. Be ashamed, be ashamed, heretic. What do you repeat that is given once? Christ is already within his members, do you not want to rebaptize him in these? For once he deigned to descend into the water with John for all (Matthew 3:16). Christ redeems souls, keeps what he redeems. Assign the whole estate to the whole Christ. Let no one invade, let no one consent to the invader: let no one wipe away the Dominican character, let no one lay down the titles of Christ. You are to give an account to the Lord the king, good servant, you have been given an opportunity to work well. Strangers, captives, and despoilers abound. Make friends out of the mammon of iniquity, so that they too may receive you into eternal tabernacles (Luke 16:9).

THE TIME OF BARBARIANS

LATIN TEXT

THE TIME OF BARBARIANS

CAPUT PRIMUM.

1. Poenitentiam amplectendam esse, cum Deus propter peccata flagellat. Flagello Dei omnes merito conteri. Admonet Dominus Deus noster, non nos debere negligere nostra peccata, quando talem demonstrat iram suam. Ipse quippe juste punit nocentem, quia nullum invenit poenitentem. Quoties, dilectissimi, intonuerunt atque intonant tubae divinae: Agite poenitentiam; appropinquavit enim ad vos regnum coelorum (Matth. IV, 17)? Et clausis auribus cordis, magis operamur mala, et petimus ut veniant bona. Sed talium judicium justum dicit esse Apostolus. In eo enim ipso quod talia sapiunt qui tales sunt, ex malis operibus posse se bona suscipere, obdurati sunt, poenitentiae locum non requirunt. Merito juste judicati, qui a semetipsis inveniuntur esse damnati. Licet non omnes tangat hic noster sermo, omnes tamen astringit sermo divinus, dicens: Omnes declinaverunt, simul inutiles facti sunt; non est qui faciat bonum, non est usque ad unum (Psal. XIII, 3). Quomodo omnes, et quomodo non omnes? Quomodo non omnes? Quia sunt multi qui gemunt et dolent ob iniquitates quae fiunt in medio eorum, volentes resistere; sed timore saecularium rerum non audentes, quas adhuc vel adipisci desiderat humana fragilitas, vel amittere formidat infirmitas. Secundum id quod dolent, non omnes: secundum quod rem non timendam timent, omnes declinaverunt, simul inutiles facti sunt; quia plus aestimatur timor hominis, quam timor Dei, et praeferunt homines res quas acceperunt a Deo ipsi Deo. Ne eas tollat malus homo, contemnitur Deus per quem factus est homo. Vellem vos quidem qui adhuc tales estis, et amore rerum saecularium obligati peccantibus aut parcitis, aut favetis; vellem vos quidem aliquibus exhortationibus admonere, quid cui rei praeponere debeatis: nisi nos fluvius lacrymarum compelleret plangere eos qui peccant, et nolunt agere poenitentiam. Si esset in nobis humanus affectus, si esset compassionis sensus, unius hominis mortem flere, dolere ac plangere deberemus: quibus lacrymis, quo gemitu, quibus planctibus exagitamur, quando aut maximam partem, aut pene totam plangimus civitatem? Aeger est charus, et vena ejus malum renuntiat; omnes qui eum diligunt, aegrotant simul animo. Si eum et in ipsa vicina morte ridere viderint, quemadmodum ab eo omnem spem salutis ablatam sentiunt, eumque adhuc vivum tanquam mortuum merito plangunt? Inter tantas angustias et in ipso fine rerum posita est universa provincia, et quotidie frequentantur spectacula: sanguis hominum quotidie funditur in

mundo, et insanientium voces crepitant in circo. O planctus omni tristitia acceptior! o planctus omni moestitia affligens cor! Libet flere. Plangimus enim, dilectissimi, et illos et nos, quia et nos digni sumus qui cum talibus merito flagellemur. Nos enim, cum alios accusamus; omnes declinavimus, simul inutiles facti sumus, prorsus omnes. Nullus est excusatus; quia talis est judex, ut omnis homo ab illo inveniatur reus. Cum enim Rex justus sederit in throno, quis gloriabitur castum se habere cor? aut quis gloriabitur mundum se esse a peccato (Prov. XX, 8 et 9)?

2. Advenit tempus illud quod praedixit Dominus: Putas, cum venerit Filius hominis, inveniet fidem in terra (Luc. XVIII, 8)? Quis habet fidem? quis credit verbis? Audebit aliquis nostrum assignare sibi fidem, quando audit Dominum dicentem discipulis: Si haberetis fidem sicut granum sinapis, diceretis arbori huic, Eradicare, et plantare in mari; et obaudisset vobis (Id. XVII, 6)? Quis sibi audebit assignare quod faciat omnia quae praecepit Deus? Nemo, prorsus nemo. Praedicamus, et non facimus: auditis, et facere non curatis. Merito omnes sub flagello, et doctor et factor, et auditor et contemptor. Studemus invicem reprehendere, et non studemus opera nostra discutere. Detrahit proximus proximo, detrahit clericus clerico, detrahit laicus laico. Video quidem se invicem accusantes, sed neminem video juste se excusantem. Unusquisque enim, dilectissimi, proprium onus portat. Nolite detrahere alterutrum, fratres, ait apostolus Jacobus. Qui enim detrahit fratri aut judicat fratrem, detrahit legi et judicat legem. Si autem judicas legem, non es factor legis, sed judex. Unus est enim legislator et judex, qui potest perdere et liberare. Tu autem quis es, qui judicas proximum (Jacobi IV, 11-13)?

CAPUT II.

3. Poenitentia agenda, antequam succidatur arbor. Nec tamen voces detrahentium silentium possunt imponere verbo Dei. Clamat ille per bonos, et per malos: Agite poenitentiam, appropinquavit ad vos regnum Dei. Nolite esse auditores legis tantum, sed factores (Jacobi I, 22). Facite dignos fructus poenitentiae. Ecce enim, ait Evangelista, securis ad radices arborum posita est. Omnis enim arbor non faciens fructum bonum, excidetur, et in ignem mittetur (Matth. III, 2, 8 et 10). Video, inquit, omnes homines diversas arbores, fructus

etiam diversos habentes: sed bonus fructus quaeritur qui pascat, non qui pungat. Sunt enim et arbores spinosae, igni deputatae, merito incendendae, quia in eis nullus fructus est animae. Putatisne, dilectissimi, nos omnes tales sumus, qui in istis malis pro peccatis nostris dimissi sumus? Exacuit agricola ferrum, amputat inutile lignum, abscisum servat incendio concremandum. Hoc nunc agitur a vero agricola. Videntur quidem sibi mali adhuc stare, adhuc florere. Quisquis talis es, quisquis malus es, quisquis corrigi non vis, non te consoletur altitudo tua; quia major te exspectat ruina, ampliorque sustinet flamma. Quia securis haec ad te nondum venit, ideo putas te posse semper stare? cum videas vel audias alias arbores te ampliores cecidisse. Quod te hic agricola differt, ejus est patientiae, ne forte intercedat apud eum locus poenitentiae. Colonus enim ille in Evangelio, qui intercedebat pro arbore, quam dominus eradicare volebat, quod fructum per triennium non haberet, videte quid ait: Domine, dimitte illam et hoc anno; faciam ei fossam, adhibeam cophinum stercoris: si fecerit fructum, bene; sin autem, abscides eam (Luc. XIII, 8, 9). Arbor haec sterilis, genus hominum est non habens fructum poenitentiae. Dominus ejus, conditor ejus est. Intercessor hujus arboris, apostolus Paulus est. Unde probamus? Audi in quadam Epistola sua quemadmodum intercedebat pro talibus: Flecto, inquit, genua mea a. Patrem Domini nostri Jesu Christi, ut det vobis virtutem (Ephes. III, 14, 16). Hoc ergo eis petebat, ut acciperent quod non habebant. Faciam, inquit, ei fossam, adhibeam cophinum stercoris. Fossa locus est humilitatis: cophinus stercoris, lacrymae sunt poenitentis. Quem locum si quis contempserit, amplius sustinebit tormentum, quando illius agricolae acutissimum senserit ferramentum. Agite, mali, poenitentiam; corrigimini, mali, quia vobiscum flagellantur et boni.

CAPUT III.

4. Quare boni cum malis puniantur. Dicet aliquis: Si mali merito flagellantur, boni quare talia cum malis et a malis patiuntur? Quare? Quia secundum quemdam modum dicuntur boni; secundum autem rectum verumque bonum, Nemo bonus, nisi solus Deus (Luc. XVIII, 19). Ergo et ipsi boni, quicumque sunt boni, non tales sunt, quales debent esse boni: non enim sunt perfectum bonum; proficiunt enim de die in diem. Si proficiunt, utique exercitationibus proficiunt. Nemo se justificet, tanquam jam sit perfectus. Recedat de medio

male justificator pelagianus, confundatur haereticus arianus: Nemo enim bonus, nisi solus Deus. Quid ergo? Christus non est Deus? Plane Deus. De ipso quippe dicit Scriptura divina: Hic est verus Deus, et vita aeterna (I Joan. V, 20). Quid Spiritus sanctus, non est Deus? Plane Deus. Unde probamus, quoniam et ipse Deus? Audi in Actibus Apostolorum Petrum Ananiae fraudatori improperantem: Anania, inquit, cur implevit satanas cor tuum, mentiri te apud Spiritum sanctum? Non es mentitus hominibus, sed Deo (Act. V, 3 et 4). Ecce et Spiritus sanctus Deus. Ergo Trinitas unus est Deus: et verum est quia nemo bonus, nisi unus Deus. Patientes estote, boni, ut sitis vere boni: patientes estote usque ad adventum Domini. Tolerate mala quae patimini a malis cum malis; quia ista tentatio, vestra est examinatio. Si aurum es, quid times paleam, quid times ignem? Simul quidem eritis in fornace, sed ignis paleas in cineres vertit, tibi sordes tollit. Si frumentum es, quid times tribulam? Non apparebis qualis antea eras in spica, nisi tribula conterendo a te separaverit paleas. Si oleum es, quid times pressuram preli? Non declarabitur species tua, nisi etiam pondus lapidis a te separaverit amurcam. Verumtamen interroget se unaquaeque anima, et videat si injuste patitur. Proferatur statera justitiae, appendatur amor mundi cum amore Dei, vide quemadmodum praeponderet amor mundi. Proferatur speculum Scripturae divinae. Speculum hoc neminem palpat: qualis es, talem te tibi demonstrat. Intende et vide, et si est aliquid quod offendat, abi confusus, et redi correctus. Annon confunderis, et in malis tuis gloriaberis? Eris enim perfectum malum, non qualecumque bonum. Talis non vis flagellari cum mundo, aut flagellatus murmuras sub flagello? Serve male, fecisti quod Dominus jussit? Ne vapulares, ista flagella tibi ante praedixit. Quis jussit? Dominus jussit, Creator tuus jussit. Quid jussit? Qui amat, inquit, patrem aut matrem plus quam me, non est me dignus. Ecce quid jussit. Aut, Qui amat filium aut filiam plusquam me, non est me dignus (Matth. X, 37). Ecce quid jussit. Et quis est, inquit, qui odit patrem aut matrem aut filios? Nec ille illos odire praecepit: sed vel quantum illos, tantum se diligi jussit. Plus quidem debueras diligere Creatorem, quam creaturam; sed si non vales praeferre, saltem vel aequare dignare. Vere filios tuos diligeres, si Christum filiis praeferres, ipsosque filios ipsi committeres. Vere filios tuos diligeres, si in ipso illos diligeres, qui eos tibi dedit ut diligas. An ideo eos videris diligere, quia eorum voluptatibus faves? Audis blasphemantes, et patienter fers, Christiane, quod rex Nabuchodonosor alienigena non potuit sustinere, dicens: Si quis dixerit blasphemiam in Deum Sidrach, Misac et Abdenago, in interitum erit (Dan. III, 96). Vides frequentare spectacula, et non revocas. Vides luxuriantes, et non verberas. Nec potes te talem exhibere patrem, qui paratus sis indisciplinatos filios vel exhaeredare vel abjicere, cum paratus esse debueras sicut Abraham etiam filium immolare. Omnis enim qui filiorum trucidat voluptates, sacrificium tale quale Abraham offert Deo. Sed dum ista non fiunt, et his moribus depravatis male nutriuntur, qui isto mundo utuntur, labefit mundus, nec immerito ait propheta: Defluxit terra, et omnes inhabitantes in ea (Isai. XXIV, 4). Non quiescunt usque nunc murmurare homines, laudare tempora praeterita, accusare tempora christiana. Magna erant tempora patrum nostrorum, dicunt: o quam bona tempora habuerunt patres nostri!

CAPUT IV.

5. Vitia quisque in suis castiget et puniat exemplo veterum. Sed videte quae fecerint patres nostri. Phinees sacrificantem virum idolis manu propria peremit, ut placaret iram Dei (Num. XXV, 8). Moyses populum oberrantem, vitulumque fusilem adorantem, ita certa emendatione coercuit, ut unam tribum e duodecim ad se vocans, quae sequi voluit Deum, praeceptum eis daret, ut acceptis gladiis in manibus suis filii percuterent parentes, et parentes occiderent filios (Exod. XXXII, 26-28). Nullus eos revocavit affectus, nullus humanitati reservatus est locus; quia timor et amor Dei prae omni desideriorum carnalium amore ferebatur. Jephte ut hostes diis ac daemonibus immolantes superaret, unicam filiam in sacrificio dedit (Judic. XI). Samson cum gentes daemonicolas, virtute quam a Deo in capite acceperat, diutius bellis contereret atque fatigaret, seductusque postea per mulierem, oculos simulque virtutem capitis perdidisset, posteaquam cognovit in opprobrium suum omnes illos convenisse ad templum idolorum suorum, eosque magnificare deos suos, quod eis tradiderant acerrimum inimicum suum, cum crescente coma capitis ejus ei crevisset et virtus, a puero qui sibi ducatum praebebat, ut sibi manum porrigeret petiit, seque ad illud templum duci poposcit. Ad quod cum pervenisset, columnas duas, supra quas totum illud aedificium ferebatur, singulis manibus singulas apprehendens, ruina se simul et illos voluit opprimi, ne laudes daemonum in contumeliam Dei sui a quoquam libenter pateretur audiri (Id. XVI). Daniel ne a rege homine petitionem aliquam posceret, sed a Deo vivo, qui praestat omnia bona suis, leonibus jejunantibus in escam datus est ut periret: sed Dominus fidelem servum suum non deserens, et ipsum intactum reservavit, et per Habacuc prophetam simul et ipsum et leones pavit

(Dan. XIV, 30-40). Quid dicam de tribus pueris, qui cum nollent imaginem regiam adorare, ignes riserunt? In quibus pueris micans gratia ita enituit, ut ligati in fornacem mitterentur, deambulantesque viderentur, os aperientes Deumque laudantes, flammas ad se non admitterent, sed fugarent: ut secum Filium Dei habere meruissent, antequam mundo in homine apparuisset; ut esset eorum vindex flamma, Chaldaeorumque ministros fornax devorans consumeret; producti quoque de fornace incolumes, populos in se mirabiles redderent, regemque mutarent, eumque facerent Dei sui adoratorem, quem senserant ante persecutorem (Id. III). Sed haec omnia faciebat fides, timor et amor Dei. Oderant isti non solum omnia quae habebant propter Deum; verum etiam animas suas: et Deus eos hic claros fecit et aeternae vitae remuneratione ditavit. Quid tale, dilectissimi, fecimus, imo e contrario quae mala non fecimus? Illi nec minis nec tormentis conventi daemoniis sacrificaverunt. Annon sacrificavit, qui imagines idolorum per noctem ludentes, quod Nocturnum vocant, libentissime spectavit? Sacrificavit, prorsus sacrificavit; et, quod est pejus, non tauri vel cujuslibet pecoris aliquam victimam, sed ipsam animam hominis pretiosam. In hoc tam nefando sacrificio non unus vel pauci accusantur; tota hoc civitas fecit, quae tota consensit. Nec ab hostibus, nec a barbaris, sed a se ipso omnis homo in anima se intus occidit videndo, consentiendo, non prohibendo; omnes remansimus rei: et dum nolumus pacem civitatis turbari perversam, pacem quam desideramus non accipimus rectam. Contemnimus pacem servare bonorum morum, et periit pax temporum nostrorum. Discite vel nunc, dilectissimi, quid cui rei praeponere debeatis. Nolite diligere vitia in filiis, in amicis, in servis, in omnibus notis. Praeponatur singularis potestas omni potestati, honorem exhibeamus Caesari tanquam Caesari, timorem autem Deo. Praeferatur Creator creaturae: diligamus Deum, quia diligit nos; et in hoc quod sic nos flagellat, diligit. Quis est enim filius, cui non det disciplinam pater ejus (Hebr. XII, 6, 7)? Qui sanam considerationem habet, qui credit Dei verbis, plus metuit ignem aeternum, quam cujuslibet truculenti barbari ferrum; plus metuit mortem perpetuam, morte qualibet hic pessima. Irrideant haec infideles, irrideant stulti, nolint credere nec rebus expertis. Ecce conteruntur, ecce omnia pereunt, ecce cum ipsis non potest stare mundus quem amaverunt, ecce ad Deum trahuntur cujus praecepta contempserunt: non enim bona voluntate pergit, qui blasphemando moritur. Ecce itur: cum illuc ventum fuerit, quid agitur? Quo itur? per quem abitur? Quis iterum huc redire cogitur? Finitum est et quod male fecerat, emendare finitum est. Redite filii, redite; redite, praevaricatores, ad cor (Isai.

XLVI, 8): facite gaudium ex conversione vestra, corrigantur corda vestra, displiceant vobis opera vestra. Estote fortes, tribulatio mundi non vos frangat: Dominus in proximo est; nihil solliciti sitis (Philipp. IV, 5 et 6).

CAPUT V.

6. Martyrum fortitudo, Perpetuae nominatim et Felicitatis. Habetis virorum fortium magna exempla. Vicerunt martyres mundum: inter quos martyres maribus etiam feminae repertae sunt fortiores. Ante paucos dies natalitia celebravimus martyrum Perpetuae et Felicitatis, et comitum. Et cum tot ibi sint viri, quare istae duae prae omnibus nominantur, nisi quia infirmior sexus aut aequavit, aut superavit virorum fortitudinem? Una earum erat praegnans, alia lactans. Felicitas parturiebat, Perpetua lactabat. Sed tamdiu haec Perpetua lactavit, quamdiu acciperet ab illo pastore simul et patre buccellam lactis: qua accepta dulcedo felicitatis perpetuae eam fecit contemnere filium, spernere patrem, non haerere mundo, perdere animam pro Christo. Felicitas vero, quae sociam habebat Perpetuam, parturiebat et dolebat, objecta bestiis gaudebat potius quam timebat. Quae virtus in feminis! Qualis est gratia, quae cum se infundit, nullum indignum judicat sexum! Gratias gratiae: reparavit enim sexum muliebrem. In opprobrium magnum mulier remanserat; quia ab initio per mulierem peccatum, et propter hanc omnes morimur. Diabolus unam Evam dejecit: sed Christus natus ex virgine, multas feminas exaltavit. Perpetua et Felicitas caput calcaverunt serpentis, quod Eva ad cor suum intus admisit. Illam seduxit falsa promittendo; illas non valuit superare saeviendo: illam decepit in paradisi felicitate; has non potuit adire, nec sub tantorum positas potestate. Illius inter paradisi delicias ruinam gavisus est; harum inter poenas fortitudinis constantiam ipse quodam modo diabolus expavit. Merito sic sunt exaltatae, merito viris vel coaequatae vel praelatae. Quamvis enim in Christo Jesu non sit servus neque liber, non sit masculus neque femina (Galat. III, 28), sed omnes sint unum occurrentes in virum perfectum (Ephes. IV, 13); descendit tamen hoc donum ex magna gratia. Perpetua enim et Felicitas nomina istarum sanctarum feminarum, merces est sanctorum omnium martyrum.

CAPUT VI.

7. Patientia Job. Vicit mundum etiam Job ille omnibus notissimus, toties tentatus, sed minime superatus. Implevit dominicum praeceptum: contempsit filios, ne blasphemaret, qui dederat filios. Repulit a se uxorem, quae ei blasphemiam persuadebat, quam diabolus propterea solam dimiserat quia sibi eam necessariam esse noverat. Non enim dimiserat marito consolatricem, sed suae tentationis adjutricem: fecerat eam Evam novam, sed ille non erat vetus Adam. Existimavit etiam istum sicut illum per mulierem posse decipere: sed iste spernendo uxorem pessima suggerentem, divinitus adjutus, etiam ipsum diabolum in illa valuit superare. Fortior fuit Job in doloribus, quam ille Adam in nemoribus: iste non cessit tormentis, ille superatus est in deliciis. Videtis, dilectissimi, quid agat tentatio, quam utiles sint hujus mundi pressurae, et quemadmodum corrumpant terrenae deliciae. Contempsit Job uxorem, filios, omnia sua, postea et carnem suam. Plus amavit eum qui dederat, quam id quod dederat. Usus est quod acceperat, tanquam bonus viator: possedit, non possessus est. At ubi ea placuit auferre qui dederat, benedixit, non blasphemavit: Dominus, inquit, dedit, et Dominus abstulit; sicut Domino placuit, ita factum est: sit nomen Domini benedictum (Job I, et II). Imitamini talem virum, imitamini tales filii esse etiam flagellati, ut mereamini recipi. Flagellat enim omnem filium quem recipit. Disciplinam ejus sustinete: sicut filios, ita vos aggreditur Deus.

CAPUT VII.

8. Parabola filii prodigi. Latus Christi apertum, ut omnes per illud intrent. Quod probat ille filius junior in Evangelio positus, qui disciplinam paternam contempsit, substantiam suam in meretricibus erogavit, porcos pavit, fame contritus est, siliquis porcorum ventrem suum implere non potuit: tandem aliquando reversus est ad se, et invenit se qui perdiderat se. In mentem ei venit quod multi mercenarii patris sui abundarent panibus, ipse vero fame periret. Statim surrexit, ad patrem recurrit, non se filium, sed tanquam unum ex servis computari rogavit. Inclinatur humilitas, excitatur misericordia: voces filii poenitentis concutiunt paterna viscera. Dicit se filius indignum, ut ille eum judicet dignum; rogat ut in numero servorum jubeatur suscipi: et pater ei

primam illam stolam jubet afferri, mactat vitulum saginatum, chorum congregat, advocat amicos, facit epulum magnum. Quare? Quia hic filius meus, inquit, mortuus fuerat, et revixit; perierat, et inventus est. Hanc similitudinem Dominus in Evangelio proposuit, quam ipse exposuit, dicens tale gaudium fieri in coelo super peccatore poenitentiam agente. Nunc vero quoniam tempus est exhortari omnes ad poenitentiam, ut filii errantes revertantur, eisque convivium a patre saginati vituli praeparetur, etiam nos, dilectissimi, parati simus huic convivio tanquam amici ac domestici interesse: maxime quia cum isto patrefamilias ad mensam ejus quotidie accedentes, non nos jam dignatur vocare servos, sed amicos. Percurramus, si placet, ipsam parabolam a Domino in Evangelio propositam, in qua nobis et affectum patris demonstravit pium, et filii perditi indicavit reditum, filiique majoris qui de paterna domo non discesserat, commotum retulit animum. Hoc quippe habet textus ipsius lectionis. Veniens, ait, filius ejus primogenitus de agro, cum audiret symphoniam, interrogavit servos quidnam illud esset: eique dixerunt, Frater tuus reversus est, et occidit illi pater tuus vitulum saginatum, eo quod salvum illum susceperit. Et indignatus noluit introire. Egressus est autem ad illum pater suus, ut eum introduceret. Improperavitque illi patri suo, quod laborasset semper cum illo, et nunquam illi talia exhibuisset: at ubi venisset filius ille, qui omnem substantiam paternam male consumpserat, occidisset illi vitulum saginatum. Et reddit pater rationem facti sui, consolaturque filium suum secum permanentem, de domo non discedentem, et dicit illi, Fili, tu meus es, et mecum es semper, et omnia mea tua sunt: verumtamen oportuit nos ista facere, quoniam frater tuus mortuus fuerat, et revixit; perierat, et inventus est (Luc. XV, 11-32). Non vacat haec talis a Domino propositio. Donet itaque nobis qui ista proposuit, ut demonstremus ab ipso fuisse impletum hoc, quod per quamdam similitudinem nos quodam modo excitavit ad aliquid inquirendum. Affectum paternum exhibuisse suis Dominum nostrum Jesum Christum, nullus ambigit christianus. Illud magis requiramus, qui sit filius junior, qui prodige vivens substantiam paternam dissipavit, et qui sit filius primogenitus qui indignatus quod filio perdito redeunti vitulus saginatus occisus sit, intrare noluerit. Quis est iste filius perditus, qui omnem substantiam paternam in meretricibus erogavit, nisi ille latro qui substantiam animae a Deo sibi datam per scelera diffluendo etiam in cruce pependit? Porcos pavit, quando daemonum voluptates suis factis implevit. Fortasse illos porcos pavit, quos petierat diabolus a Domino, dicens: Jube nos intrare in gregem porcorum (Matth. VIII, 31). Fame contritus est, quia panem verbi Dei non inveniebat.

Siliquis cupiebat saturare ventrem suum, quando tortuosis cogitationibus replebat animam suam. Sed revertatur ad se, videat se latro in cruce pendentem, concurrat ad patrem, dicat pendens in cruce: Domine, memento mei dum veneris in regnum tuum. Domine, memento mei; non sum dignus vocari filius tuus, suscipe me tanquam unum ex servis. Domine, memento mei. Latro enim sua attendens merita de se ipso diffidebat: sed Dominus, tanquam pius pater, latroni quasi filio quod desperaverat offerebat. Proferat huic pater stolam illam primam, induat filium immortalitate, quem secum videt in cruce pendentem, introducat eum in domum: dicat Christus latroni, Amen dico tibi, hodie mecum eris in paradiso (Luc. XXIII, 42, 43). Mactet vitulum saginatum, hominem illum susceptum, etiam pro latronibus crucifixum: advocet amicos suos discipulos quibus dicebat, Si feceritis quae mando vobis, jam vos non dicam servos, sed amicos (Joan. XV, 14 et 15). Praeparetur illud convivium coeleste, astet ille chorus Angelorum, suaviter declamans: Gloria in excelsis Deo, et in terra pax hominibus bonae voluntatis (Luc. II, 14). Veniat et primogenitus filius ille, et nolit intrare. Quis est iste filius primogenitus qui noluit intrare, nisi ille primus Apostolorum Petrus, qui ad interrogationem unius ancillae in atrio sacerdotis ter Dominum ausus est negare? Dixisti quidem, o Petre, tanquam patri tuo Christo, Ego tecum laboravi: quando dicebas Salvatori, Tecum sum usque ad mortem (Matth. XXVI, 69-74, 35); animam meam pro te ponam (Joan. XIII, 37). Ubi est quod promisisti? Interrogaris semel, et negas: secundo interrogaris, et negas; tertio, et negas. Non vis ad convivium intrare, ideo ausus es ter Dominum negare. Ubi est, Animam meam pro te ponam? Ter negantem non terruit ungula, sed una oppressit muliercula. Certe, Tecum sum usque ad mortem. Vide, vide igitur, Petre, quantum de te antea praesumpseris: ecce nunc ter negando, gallo teste convinceris. Sed egrediatur pater ad primogenitum filium nolentem intrare: dicat Christus Petro, Intra in gaudium Domini tui (Matth. XXV, 21). Respiciat negantem, et faciat confessorem: compungat flentem, faciat amatorem. Exhortetur eum paterna voce: Fili, inquit, tu meus es: Tu es Petrus; etsi me negasti, meus es. Tu es Petrus, et super hanc petram aedificabo Ecclesiam meam. Tu meus es, et omnia mea tua sunt: Tibi dabo claves regni coelorum (Id. XVI, 18, 19). Apud te, Petre, sunt claves: dignare jam ad convivium intrare. Oportebat haec fieri, quoniam frater tuus latro mortuus erat, et revixit; perierat, et inventus est. Si Petrus antequam Christus pro omnibus crucifigeretur, regni coelorum claves accepit; qua illuc introivit latro ille jam non reus, nisi per latus quod aperuit Judaeus?

9. Et nunc veniant omnes quicumque amant paradisum, locum quietis, locum securitatis, locum perpetuae felicitatis, locum in quo non pertimescas barbarum, in quo nullum patiaris adversarium, nullum habeas inimicum: venite omnes, intrate omnes; est qua intrare possitis, patet latus. Ostendit enim ille latro quo debeant omnes intrare, neminem suo exemplo docuit desperare.

CAPUT VIII.

De cavenda ariana haeresi.--Contendite, ait Dominus, intrare per angustam portam (Luc. XIII, 24). Quid angustius illo foramine, quod unus e militibus percutiendo latus crucifixi aperuit? et tamen per has angustias pene jam totus mundus intravit. Venite, et vos Judaei, vocat vos quem crucifixistis Filius Dei. Contendite intrare per angustam portam: per hanc enim introierunt patres vestri. Illi qui ut crucifigeretur clamaverunt, qui in ligno suspensum viderunt, qui irriserunt, qui caput agitaverunt, per istas tamen angustias introierunt. Non enim inaniter clamabat ille pendens in cruce: Pater, ignosce illis, quia nesciunt quid faciunt (Id. XXIII, 34). Per has ergo, ut dixi, angustias, per angustam portam lateris Christi ingressus est latro mutatus, poenitens Judaeus, conversus omnis paganus, et ab eo exiit foras malus haereticus arianus. Exiit, quoniam non erat de numero permanentium. De illis enim erat, de quibus Joannes dicit: Ex nobis exierunt, sed non erant ex nobis: si enim ex nobis essent, mansissent utique nobiscum (I Joan. II, 19). O haeretice ariane, agnoscit latro in cruce pendentem, ipsi inimici Judaei expaverunt resurgentem, et vos male tractatis in coelo regnantem!

10. Cavete, dilectissimi, arianam pestem; non vos separent a Christo terrena promittendo, propter tunicam non vos exspolient fide. Membra Christi, servate unitatem atque integritatem unius tunicae, quam nec persecutores Christi ausi sunt scindere. Nolite injurias irrogare capiti vestro: pro vobis ille mortuus est, ne vos moreremini. Quem Christus per Baptismum vivificavit, quare eum arianus rebaptizando occidit? Erubesce, erubesce, haeretice. Negavit Petrus, et reversus est, et flendo delevit quod timore negavit. Christum in suis persecutus est Paulus, sed ad ejus vocem cecidit et surrexit. Aliter cecidit, aliter surrexit: cecidit persecutor, erectus est praedicator. In Christianis Christum persecuti sunt reges: sed multum eis praestiterunt, quando membra ad caput

suum velociter transierunt. Nemo talia damna, qualia tu, ingerit Christo: animas enim multorum cupis interficere, pro quibus Christus in carne venit occidi. Erubesce, erubesce, haeretice. Quid iteras quod semel datur? In membris suis jam intus est Christus, noli in istis ipsum velle rebaptizare? Semel enim pro omnibus cum Joanne in aquam dignatus est ipse descendere (Matth. III, 16). Redemit Christus animas, custodite quod ille redemit. Integro Christo integrum assignate praedium. Nemo invadat, nemo invasori consentiat: characterem dominicum nullus abstergat, titulos Christi nemo deponat. Reddituri estis rationem Domino regi, boni servi, data est vobis occasio bene operandi. Abundant peregrini, captivi, exspoliati. Facite vobis amicos ex mammona iniquitatis, ut et ipsi recipiant vos in tabernacula aeterna (Luc. XVI, 9).

The Scriptorium Project is the work of a small group of lay people of various apostolic churches who are interested in the preservation, transmission, and translation of the works of the early and medieval church. Our efforts are to make the works of the church fathers accessible to anyone who might have an interest in Christian antiquities and the theological, philosophical, and moral writings that have become the bedrock of Western Civilization.

To-date, our releases have pulled from the Greek, Syriac, Georgian, Latin, Celtic, Ethiopian, and Coptic traditions of Christianity, and have been pulled from sundry local traditions and languages.